Careers in Virtual Reality Technology

Joshua Gregory

Published in the United States of America by
Cherry Lake Publishing, Ann Arbor, Michigan
www.cherrylakepublishing.com

Reading Adviser: Marla Conn, MS, Ed., Literacy specialist, Read-Ability, Inc.

Photo Credits: Cover, Mark Nazh/Shutterstock; page 4 (left), eHrach/Shutterstock, (right) Riksa Prayogi/
Shutterstock; page 6, Lukas Gojka/Shutterstock; page 8, Alphaspirit/Shutterstock; page 10, Iakov Filimonov/
Shutterstock; page 12, GRandeDuc/Shutterstock; page 14, KeongDaGreat/Shutterstock; page 16, Karramba
Production/Shutterstock; page 18, Africa Studios/Shutterstock; page 20, Kikiiy/Shutterstock; page 22,
g-stockstudio/Shutterstock; page 24, Supamotion/Shutterstock; page 26, Photographee.eu/Shutterstock;
page 28, vectorfusionart/Shutterstock.

Library of Congress Cataloging-in-Publication Data

CIP data has been filed and is available at catalog.loc.gov.

Printed in the United States of America.

Table of Contents

Hello, Emerging Tech Careers!

In the past ...
Groundbreaking inventions made life easier in many ways.

In the present ...
New technologies are changing the world in mind-boggling ways.

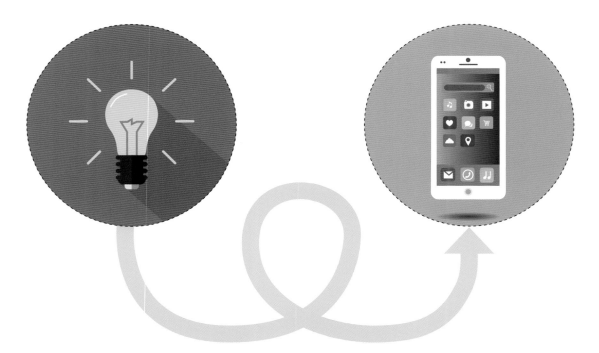

The future is yours to imagine!

WHAT COMES NEXT?

Who would have thought?

Alexander Graham Bell invented the first telephone in 1876. In 1879, Thomas Edison invented the first electric lightbulb. The Wright brothers successfully flew the first airplane in 1903. And don't forget Henry Ford! He invented a way to make cars quicker and cheaper.

These brilliant inventors did things that people once thought were impossible. To go from candles to electricity? From horse-drawn carriages to automobiles and airplanes? Wow!

The sky's the limit!

Now technology is being used to do even more amazing things! Take **virtual reality**, for instance. Virtual reality is a life-like, computer-generated environment in which a person can explore and interact. It is being used to create some amazing games. It is also being used to provide training **simulations** used by the military, in medicine, and other types of businesses.

This book explores the people and professions behind virtual reality. Creating realistic worlds for both fun and business is adding an exciting new twist to careers like game designer and hardware engineer.

Read on to explore exciting possibilities for your future!

3D
Animator

Leaves sway in the breeze. The beam of your virtual flashlight makes wet rocks sparkle. A virtual dog trots alongside you, wagging its tail. Just like a real dog, it sits and starts scratching itself with a kicking motion. It all seems so real, but it is only very realistic **animation**.

Animation plays a major role in making a virtual world seem lifelike. If there was no movement in the virtual scenes you were seeing, then the experience would feel strange and unrealistic.

Think about your real-life experiences. Even in a still, peaceful environment, there is movement all around you. Wind makes plants sway. Dirt and dust blow along the ground. The light around you changes as clouds move in front of the sun. Even if you try to sit perfectly still, your body moves as you breathe.

In a virtual world, all the movement you see is created by skilled animators. These professionals use a variety of techniques to bring **3D** models to life. For example, sometimes they might take a 3D model of a character and create each of its movements by hand. They would determine how its legs need to bend and move for each step it takes, how its head turns, and more. Each movement requires its own image.

Imagine It!

● Watch a friend or relative carefully as he or she moves around.

● What do you notice about the person's movements? What do the movements tell you about the person's mood or personality?

● Use a smartphone to take a quick **sequence** of photos. Notice the tiny differences among each image.

Dig Deeper!

● Google's Toontastic 3D app is a great way to get started with 3D animation. Check it out at https://toontastic.withgoogle.com.

● Ask an adult to help you download the app to a tablet or smartphone.

Watch out! Virtual reality makes even dinosaurs appear real.

Another technique that is commonly used in computer **graphics** today is called **motion capture**. Animators hire actors to wear suits with special devices attached to certain points on the body. As the actor moves around, animators use a computer to record the movements of the devices on the suit. They then map the movements to matching points on a 3D model.

Animation is more than just making characters move. Animators also determine the way a virtual explosion will affect the virtual objects around it or how a virtual flag flaps in the wind.

Animators sometimes specialize in one specific type of movement. For example, one might be especially good at creating more realistic movement for virtual hair. Another might be an expert in the way facial expressions are animated. The level of detail involved in animation is mind-boggling. Making each move as realistic as possible is what virtutal reality is all about.

Future 3D Animator

3D animators must be both technically skilled and highly creative. In addition to being experienced with a variety of animation **software**, animators often need a strong understanding of math and physics. This means many jobs in 3D animation require a college degree. But if you're interested in animation, there's no reason you can't start learning today. Grab a notebook and start sketching everything you see!

3D Artist

Like 3D animators, 3D artists work to create virtual worlds. The difference: Animators work on movement and special effects. Artists create realistic characters and environments.

Advances in computer graphics are a big part of the reason VR has become more popular in recent years. Have you ever played a really old video game? You probably noticed that it doesn't look very realistic. But in today's video games and movies, computer graphics are so good that it is sometimes hard to tell what is and isn't real.

One reason computer graphics are so good today is simply that computers are more powerful than they used to be. But as we know, computers can only do what people tell them to do. The makers of games and other VR experiences take advantage of today's powerful computers by creating detailed, beautiful 3D graphics.

Everything you see as you explore a virtual world is the creation of talented 3D artists. This includes everything from the virtual characters you meet to the buildings you explore and the sky above you.

To create a 3D object for a virtual world, artists often start by sketching ideas

Imagine It!

- Sketch some ideas for characters for a VR game on paper.

- Think carefully about the characters' appearances. How will players feel when they see the characters? Are the characters friendly? Scary? Funny?

- Be creative. Don't be afraid to try weird ideas!

Dig Deeper!

- Get started designing your own 3D models. Ask an adult to help you use Tinkercad, a free 3D modeling program, at https://www.tinkercad.com.

- Another popular choice for beginners is SketchUp. You can get started at https://www.sketchup.com/products/sketchup-free.

3-D artists must pay attention to every detail to make realistic images.

on paper. Once they have a rough idea in mind, they can start building a 3D model. To do this, they use software such as Maya or 3DS Max. A 3D model is built from shapes called **polygons**. The more detailed a model is, the more polygons it is likely to be made from. For example, a character in one of the latest video games or movies might be made of millions of tiny shapes.

Even once a 3D model has a finished shape, it is not quite finished. It has a plain, uncolored appearance. 3D artists must add a texture to the outside of the model. A texture is like a skin that contains all of the color and other details on the outside of an object.

The finished 3D models are pieced together and arranged to form the virtual worlds you explore in a VR experience. Artists add light sources, fog, and other important visual effects to the world to make it even more realistic. As computer graphics technology continues to improve, 3D artists will be able to create even more lifelike graphics, making VR experiences seem even more real.

Future 3D Artist

The artists who make 3D graphics for VR games need both creative and technical skills to succeed. Most 3D artists attend college to help them become experts in the software they need to do the job. But they usually have a natural passion for art. If you love to draw pictures and make up your own unique characters and settings, this could be the perfect job for you.

Game Designer

Have you ever wondered what it would be like to live inside your favorite video game? You don't have to wonder anymore. Virtual reality (VR) is changing the way people play video games. Instead of looking at a screen, you can jump into a whole new world!

Some VR experiences are simply 3D worlds where you can move around and look at things. But many of today's most popular and interesting VR programs are full-fledged video games. There are VR games where you can drive high-speed race cars or explore detailed fantasy worlds. There are even VR games where you can become Batman or fly a *Star Wars* ship.

A huge number of elements go into the creation of a single VR game. There are the graphics and sound. There are the game's controls. There are rules for players to follow and goals for them to achieve. In many games, there are stories, characters, and dialogue, just like a movie or TV show. So, who oversees all of this to make sure it fits together as a fun game?

Game designers! They are the creative thinkers behind all your favorite games. Sometimes they work alone or as part of a small team. Other times, they work alongside hundreds of other people to

Imagine It!

➡ Try designing your own game. It could be a board game, a card game, or even an idea for a video game.

➡ What will be the player's goal?

➡ What obstacles will the player face along the way? Are there rules to follow? Enemies to defeat?

Dig Deeper!

✔ The best way to get ideas for new games is to play games created by others.

✔ Check out some of the games kids have made using Scratch at https://scratch.mit.edu/explore/projects/games.

Some virtual reality games put players in the driver's seat!

get the job done. Often, a lead designer oversees several smaller teams that each work on separate parts of the game.

Designers are always thinking about ways to make a game more interesting or fun to play. They plan out exciting levels for players to explore. They come up with unique settings and stories for their games. They think about new ways of controlling a game.

A designer's job is more than just dreaming up fun games, though. Game designers have to figure out whether their ideas are even possible with current technology. They also have to consider their projects' budgets. Sometimes a great idea for a game might simply be too expensive to create.

Most game designers have technical skills as well as creative talent. Their knowledge of programming and game design software helps them communicate with other team members.

Future Game Designer

It can be tough for new designers to get a foot in the door at big VR game companies. Video games are very popular, and there are a lot of people who want to help make them. One way to improve your chances of getting a job is to work on your own small game design projects. You never know who your creations might impress!

Hardware Engineer

You can't believe what you're seeing and hearing. An enormous dinosaur is crashing through the trees next to you! Rushing to escape, you activate your jetpack and zoom high above the forest. Suddenly, you hear your dad calling you to dinner. You take off your new VR headset and find yourself back in your living room.

Virtual reality (VR) devices allow users to feel like they have been transported into new worlds. Everything the users see, hear, and even touch seems like it is really there. The things you can touch are made possible by hardware engineers.

Some VR devices are as simple as a cardboard headset that holds a smartphone screen in front of the user's eyes. Other VR hardware is far more **complex**. A typical VR headset has video screens to change what people will see and headphones to change what they hear. Sensors detect users' head movements. This makes them feel like they are really looking around.

Many VR sets come with special controllers for users to hold. These controllers contain motion sensors much like the ones that track head movements. This allows users to move their arms in the virtual world. Some VR sets also have sensors that can be placed around a room. They can track the users' movements as they walk around.

Imagine It!

➡ Brainstorm ideas for a new VR headset. Draw a picture of the device and label the different parts.

➡ Remember that users have to wear the headset. Don't make it too big or heavy!

➡ Look at other VR headsets online to get ideas.

Dig Deeper!

✔ The best way to understand how VR works is to try it yourself.

✔ If you don't have your own VR equipment, visit an electronics store. Many have VR setups available to try.

Hardware engineers develop new ways to experience virtual reality.

Even the simplest VR device is packed full of advanced technology. Sensors, video screens, and speakers are just a start. So, who figures out how all these pieces fit together?

Hardware engineers who work for VR companies design and build the hardware that people use to experience virtual reality. They figure out which parts are needed and how they will work together. They also make sure a VR device is comfortable easy to use, and that it looks nice.

Engineers might start a new project by sketching their ideas on paper. They build early versions called prototypes. By testing a prototype, they can see which ideas are working and which ones need improvement. They keep making better and better prototypes. This process can take years of hard work and experimentation. Finally, the completed version is manufactured and released for people to buy.

Future Hardware Engineer

The field of VR technology is growing quickly. VR hardware companies need creative thinkers with a strong knowledge of technology. If you want to help design the latest VR equipment, you'll likely need a college degree. You will also have an easier time finding a job if you have some experience building and tinkering with your own homemade tech projects.

Programmer

Stars rush outside your cockpit window as you jet through space at light speed. This new virtual reality (VR) spaceship game is a ton of fun. But suddenly, everything goes black. You no longer hear the roar of your ship's engines. What went wrong? Your VR software has crashed!

There are two main parts to any VR experience: hardware and software. Hardware is all the equipment you need to explore a virtual world. It includes headsets and game controllers. It also includes the smartphone, desktop computer, or game console you plug your VR devices into.

Software is any computer program that makes hardware work. It controls everything you see and hear when you are using a VR device. For example, when you turn your head, the sensors in your VR hardware measure how much you moved and which direction you moved in. The sensors feed the movement information into a computer program. The program then uses this information to determine what you should be seeing on the headset's video screens. This is software at work. The program sends the new images to your headset's video screens. All of this happens instantly and continuously. If all goes well, you never have to think about the hardware or software while you enjoy VR.

Imagine It!

● Pretend you are programming a computer to do something you do every day, such as brushing your teeth.

● Create a chart explaining every step you need to follow to complete this activity.

● Be as detailed as possible. Which direction do you move the toothbrush? How long do you brush?

Dig Deeper!

● Learn the basics of programming with Scratch. Ask an adult to help you get started at https://scratch.mit.edu.

● You can also learn coding with games created with Google's Blockly coding system. Visit https://blockly-games.appspot.com.

Programmers write the code that make virtual reality happen.

Computer software is created by workers called programmers. They create instructions for computers and other hardware to follow. Computers are powerful, but they cannot think for themselves. They need to be told exactly how to respond in any situation. That's what programmers do.

Programmers write instructions, or code, using special languages that computers can understand. Like the languages humans use to communicate with each other, programming languages have many rules to follow. Each programming language is a little bit different. Knowing which one to use in which situation is part of being a good programmer.

Good software is necessary for a smooth, convincing VR experience. Programmers test their software over and over again to make sure it works correctly. An important part of the job is fixing any "bugs" before the program is released.

Future Programmer

Skilled computer programmers are always in high demand at tech companies. Most have college degrees. However, the most important thing a programmer needs is coding skills. Many successful programmers start learning how to code when they are very young. They create their own simple programs and experiment with new programming languages. Programmers never stop learning new things. They always need to keep up with the latest languages.

Research Scientist

Watch science-fiction movies from the 1980s and 1990s, You might be surprised to see people using virtual reality (VR) devices that are very similar to the ones available today. Is virtual reality really that old? Why did you only start hearing about it over the past few years?

While VR has taken the world by storm recently, it is not a brand-new invention. Engineers, scientists, and other experts have been working on VR technology for decades.

Scientists first started trying to build VR headsets in the 1960s. The U.S. military and the National Aeronautics and Space Administration wanted this technology for use in **simulators** for pilots and astronauts. But what scientists produced were large, heavy, and far less powerful than even the most basic VR headset sold today.

In the 1980s, many scientists and inventors started to get more excited by the possibilities of VR technology. This is when the term *virtual reality* was first used. Forward-thinking inventors created better VR headsets, motion-tracking gloves, and other technology similar to the kinds used today. However, these devices were simply too expensive for the average person to afford. Computers of the time were also not powerful enough to create realistic virtual worlds.

Imagine It!

- Choose one type of VR technology that you are most interested in—for example, display screens, motion controls, or computer graphics.

- Make a list of questions you have about how this technology works.

- Think of an experiment you could do to answer each question.

Dig Deeper!

- Learn more about the history and science behind virtual reality at https://www.fi.edu/virtual-reality/history-of-virtual-reality.

- Keep up with some of the latest developments in VR tech at https://www.wired.com/tag/virtual-reality.

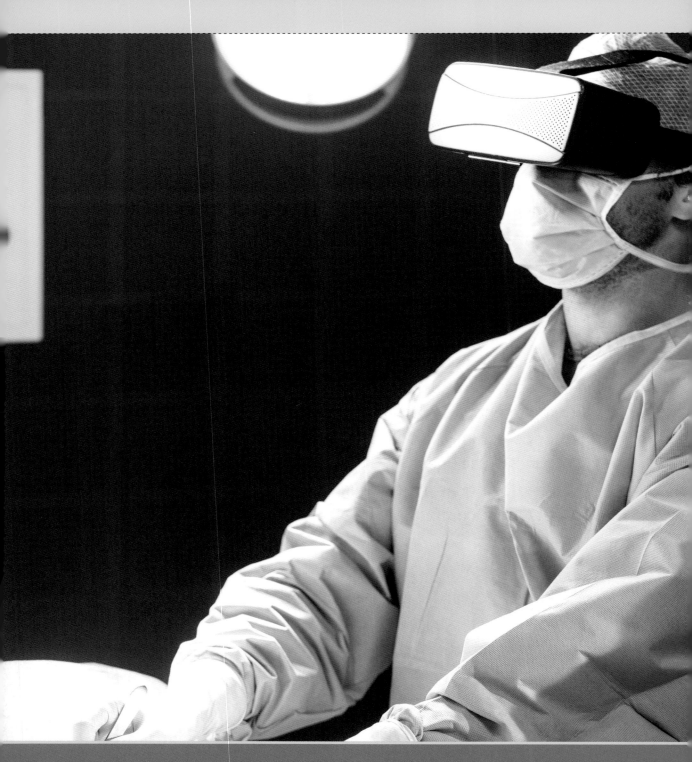

Virtual reality is also used to help train people for real jobs like performing surgery.

By the 2010s, VR technology was more powerful than ever before. It was also inexpensive and lightweight enough for many people to enjoy at home.

Research scientists are among the leading experts in this field. They conduct experiments in labs to find new ways of pushing technology forward. As they make discoveries and learn new things, they share their knowledge with engineers and other experts. These innovators can then use the scientists' findings to create better VR technology.

Scientists at VR companies usually focus on researching one specific area of VR tech. For example, one person might work on trying to find a way to improve the quality of video screens. Another person might look for ways to prevent VR users from getting motion sickness. In a different lab, scientists might experiment with new types of lightweight plastic to make headsets more comfortable.

Future Research Scientist

To become a VR research scientist, you'll need a lot of education and experience. Most jobs require a **PhD**. They also require years of experience working with the latest technology. However, all this hard work will pay off. Scientists with a proven record of conducting unique, interesting research will have no trouble finding work at the industry's top companies.

Can You Imagine?

Innovation always starts with an idea. This was true for Alexander Graham Bell, Thomas Edison, Henry Ford, and the Wright brothers. It is still true today as innovators imagine new ways to use virtual reality. And it will still be true in the future when you begin your high-tech career. So ...

What is your big idea?

Think of a cool way to use virtual reality. Write a story or draw a picture to share your idea with others.

Please do **NOT** write in this book if it doesn't belong to you.
Gather your own paper and art supplies and get creative with your ideas!

Glossary

3D (THREE-DEE) images that seem to have the three dimensions—length, width, and height—that create realistic scenes in virtual reality

animation (an-uh-MAY-shuhn) the use of drawings, models, or objects posed that are arranged so that when shown in rapid sequence, they look like real-life motion

complex (KAHM-pleks) difficult to do or understand because of having a large number of parts

graphics (GRAF-iks) images such as drawings or maps

motion capture (MOH-shuhn KAP-chur) the process of recording patterns of movement digitally, especially the recording of an actor's movements for the purpose of animating a character in a movie or video game

PhD (PEE AYCH DEE) the highest college degree, awarded to a person who has done advanced research in a particular subject; also called a doctorate

polygons (PAH-lih-gahnz) shapes with three or more straight sides

sequence (SEE-kwuhns) a series of things that follow one another in a particular order

simulations (sim-yuh-LAY-shunhns) trial runs to act out real events

simulators (SIM-yuh-lay-tur) a machine that allows a person to experience or perform a complex task, such as flying a plane, by imitating the conditions and controls

software (SAWFT-wair) computer programs that control computer equipment and tell it to do specific tasks

virtual reality (VUR-choo-uhl ree-AL-ih-tee) a computer-created environment that looks and seems real to the person who experiences it

Index

About the Author

Joshua Gregory is the author of more than 125 books for young readers. He currently lives in Chicago, Illinois.